GEYSERS

GEYSERS
When Earth Roars

Roy A. Gallant

A First Book

Franklin Watts   A Division of Grolier Publishing
New York • London • Hong Kong • Sydney • Danbury, Connecticut

For Max

Expert consultant: Samuel Storch

Photographs ©: Al Giddings Images: 35, 36, 38; Peter Arnold Inc.: 31 (John Cancalosi), 29 (Kevin Schafer), 52 (Clyde H. Smith), 18 (Jim Wark); Photo Researchers: back cover, 24 (Simon Fraser/SPL), 15 (David Halpern), 16 (Jeff Leopold), 2 (J. H. Robinson), cover (C. Seghers), 48 (Jim Steinberg); Roy A. Gallant: 6, 10, 11, 64; Wolfgang Käehler: 27; Yellowstone National Park: 19, 20, 22.

Library of Congress Cataloging-in-Publication Data
Gallant, Roy A.
    Geysers: when Earth roars / Roy A. Gallant
       p. cm. — (A first book)
    Includes bibliographical references and index.
    Summary: Discusses various aspects of geysers including their formation, location, anatomy, use by humans, and extinction.
      ISBN 0-531-20288-7 (lib.bdg.) 0-531-15838-1 (pbk.)
      1. Geysers—Juvenile literature. [1. Geysers.] I. Title.
II. Series.
    GB1198.5.G35 1997
    551.2'3—dc20   96-33306
                                     CIP
                                     AC

CONTENTS

Mount Karymsky is one of the most active volcanoes in Russia's Kamchatka Peninsula.

One

Kamchatka's Valley of Geysers

My gaze was fixed on a gray plume of steam gently rising out of the crater atop Mount Karymsky. The mountain is one of Russia's most active volcanoes. Only about a 30-minute hike away, the smoothly sloping lines of the 5,040-foot- (1,536-m-) high cone towered above me. This volcano was very much alive.

"No, it's not going to erupt today, if that's what you're wondering." The voice was that of Dr. Vladimir Kirianov, a volcano scientist at the Institute of Geology and Geochemistry in Russia. The Institute is located on the Kamchatka Peninsula, which is part of Siberia. Kamchatka is also the home of 29 active volcanoes and more than 300 extinct ones. That makes it the most active section of the *Pacific Rim of Fire*.

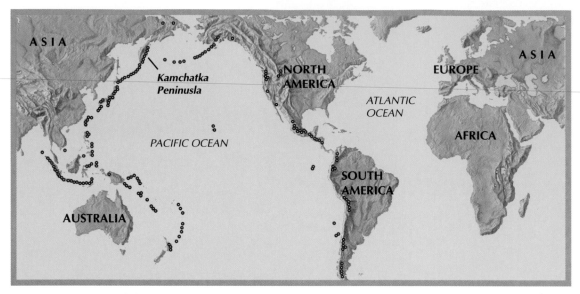

Most of the world's active volcanoes are found along the edges of the Pacific Ocean. This area is often called the Pacific Rim of Fire.

"Maybe not today," I answered, looking at my red-bearded friend, "but maybe next week . . . next month?"

He shrugged and smiled. *"Moshebuit"* (Russian for "maybe"). Over the past 200 years, Karymsky has erupted 21 times. Little did I know that only 3 months after my expedition, the mountain would erupt again.

Why have I begun a book about *geysers* by talking about a volcano? Where there are volcanoes, there are usually geysers. In fact, the real purpose of my trip to the Kamchatka Peninsula was to visit Kronotski National Park, which has a famous valley of geysers called Dolina Geizerov. This valley, with its steep mountain walls, is part of a young and active volcanic area. It is energized by a layer of hot liquid rock deep

8

beneath the ground. This layer of rock is associated with Kikhpinych Volcano, which last erupted in the 1890s.

One-quarter of the world's geysers—some 200—are in this remarkable valley. Velikan, which means "the Giant," gushes steam and water to a height of 180 feet (55 m). Troynoy, which means "Triple," sends a majestic arching spray more than 100 feet (30 m) into the air. Malyi, which means "Little," spouts to a height of 70 feet (21 m) every 40 minutes.

There are also dozens of smaller geysers that spew steam just a few feet into the air. Others reach a height of only a few inches. Wherever you turn, you can count at least a dozen geysers. They hiss, roar, and gurgle in a hot-rock concert.

One of the most memorable sights in the valley is an enormous green wall of geysers called Grot Yubileinyi, which means "Jubilee Grotto." A grotto is a structure that looks like a cave.

This geyser's spectacular coloring comes from heat-loving bacteria that make their home in boiling water. Like all geysers, Jubilee Grotto's activity changes over time.

Sometimes, the geyser sends steam and water exploding some 230 feet (70 m) into the air. When I was there it was active, but not wildly so. It has been known to erupt every 3 minutes with as many as seven outbursts in a row. Such violent activity is bound to change the area around the Grotto over time, but that is the nature of geysers.

Geysers galore continuously erupt throughout Kamchatka's remarkable Valley of Geysers. Some 200 of them hiss, roar, gurgle, and plop as mudpots.

The World's Biggest Geyser Field

I n Iceland they're called "gazirs," which means "to gush." The English call them "geezers." In the United States, they're called geysers. However you pronounce them, they are one of nature's wonders.

A geyser is one type of natural *hot spring*. It is different from other hot springs because it erupts with a gush of steam and water from time to time. There are about 800 geysers in the world, and Yellowstone National Park has half of them. It is also the home of some 10,000 steam vents, bubbling mud pots, and quiet hot springs.

An underground "plumbing system" of natural tubes and caverns is a geyser's fuel tank, and water is its fuel. Before a geyser can spout, a few things must happen. First of all, the water in its underground network must be heated.

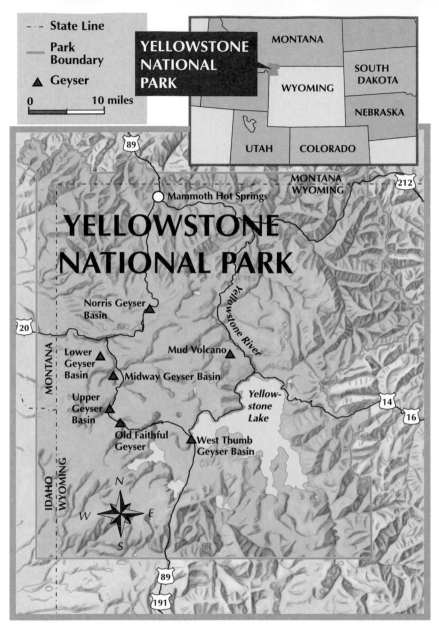

YELLOWSTONE NATIONAL PARK

MONTANA

WYOMING

SOUTH DAKOTA

NEBRASKA

UTAH   COLORADO

89

MONTANA
WYOMING

212

Mammoth Hot Springs

YELLOWSTONE
NATIONAL PARK

20

MONTANA

Norris Geyser
Basin

Mud Volcano ▲

Yellowstone River

Lower
Geyser
Basin ▲

▲ Midway Geyser Basin

Upper
Geyser
Basin ▲

Yellow-
stone
Lake

14

16

Old Faithful
Geyser

▲ West Thumb
Geyser Basin

IDAHO
WYOMING

N
W   E
S

89

191

Half of all the geysers in the world are located in Yellowstone National Park in the United States. Most of the park is in Wyoming, but the western border is in Idaho and the northern border is in Montana.

Yellowstone's natural "hot plate" is an underground pool of molten rock called *magma*. This soupy rock layer, which is located about 3 miles (5 km) beneath Yellowstone, boils any water that comes near it.

Kinds of Geysers

What happens to the heated water when it reaches the surface depends on the size and shape of the tubes that make up a particular hot spring's plumbing system. In some cases, the water will form a quiet pool. In other cases, it will occasionally spring to life and blast hundreds of feet into the air. This type of hot spring is called a geyser.

Some geysers are regular, meaning that they erupt more or less on schedule. Old Faithful is a regular geyser. In 1996, it exploded once every 77 minutes; in 1970, it erupted once every 66 minutes. Over time, Old Faithful seems to be running out of steam.

Most geysers are irregular, meaning that their eruptions can't be predicted very well. This is because their underground plumbing system is shared with one or more other hot springs. Yellowstone's Daisy Geyser and neighboring Bonita Pool are good examples of irregular geysers.

Most of the time, Daisy spews a 3-minute-long, 75-foot- (23-m-) high fountain of water and steam once every 1.5 to

Is Yellowstone's famous geyser Old Faithful becoming "Old Unfaithful"? The length of time between eruptions seems to be gradually growing longer.

3 hours. Meanwhile, nearby Bonita Pool just quietly floods and overflows. But there are periods when the energy of this twin system is shifted to favor Bonita Pool. At such times, Bonita overflows heavily with frequent small eruptions while Daisy erupts only once in a while. This shift in geyser activity may last several years.

Yellowstone also has many sleeping geysers. One of the most remarkable is Excelsior Geyser—a crater about 200 × 300 feet (60 × 90 m) deep. This geyser spills out 250,000 gallons (950,000 l) of boiling water an hour and produces great clouds of steam.

Yellowstone's Excelsior Geyser spews 250,000 gallons (950,000 l) of boiling water an hour into the Firehole River. Colorful algae beds grace the edges of the runoff channels.

Some geysers spew mud rather than water. Yellowstone's most famous *mud geyser* is Black Dragon's Cauldron. It blows every few seconds and sends a 9-foot- (3-m-) high tower of mud skyward.

The Beauty of Geysers

Between eruptions, a geyser looks like any other hot spring or pool. Many are a deep blue color. The spring or pool looks blue for the same reason the sky looks blue. When the sun shines, it gives off white light. This white light can be separated into all the colors of the rainbow. When white light hits the air or water, the blue light is bounced around by the air or water particles and scattered in all directions. So it is mostly the blue portion of the sun's white light that hits our eyes. That is why we see blue when we look at the sky or most hot springs and pools.

Some pools are an intense blue-green. We see this color whenever the pool contains microscopic organisms called *algae* or a yellow mineral called sulfur. In these pools, the blue light from the sun mixes with yellow algae or sulfur to produce a blue-green color.

Yellow algae line the craters of any geyser with water between 155 and 164°F (68 and 73°C). If the temperature of the spring is just a few degrees cooler, the algae will be

17

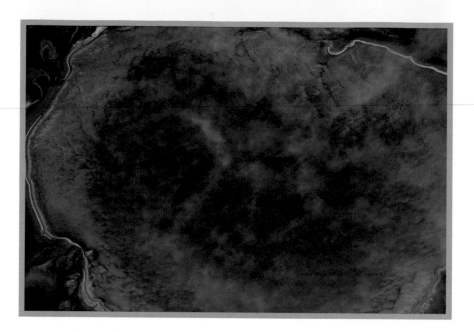

Colorful pools, like Yellowstone's Fountain Paint Pot, are a bright blue-green color. This color is caused by blue light from the sky mixing with yellow algae or sulfur in the water.

orange-brown, not yellow. Brilliantly tinted, heat-loving algae and *bacteria* are responsible for the stunningly colorful geysers found in Yellowstone's Lower Geyser Basin.

If you were to walk along one of the outlet channels of a geyser, you'd notice something pretty amazing. You'd see that the color of the water changes from place to place. Because the water cools as it travels farther and farther away from the geyser, the color changes show that different kinds of organisms prefer different water temperatures. In fact, you can use the different-colored organisms as natural thermometers.

If you see stringy, pale-yellow or pink strands of bacteria, the water temperature is above 180°F (82°C). Farther down the channel, yellow algae mark a temperature around 158°F (70°C). Next come bright orange algae. The water they live in is about 145°F (63°C). As you move even farther from the geyser, you will see dark brown organisms. They indicate a temperature of about 129°F (54°C). When the water cools to about 122°F (50°C), you will see green algae.

Multicolored hot springs in Yellowstone are home to "living thermometers." These are pink, yellow, orange, or brown bacteria and algae, each living in water of a certain temperature.

Exquisite mineral formations are abundant throughout Yellowstone's geyser fields. Red and orange-yellow structures indicate the presence of arsenic. Popcornlike bunches of white and yellow minerals coat the gravel found along barren flats.

Other formations are made of a flaky, brittle material called *geyserite*, which contains the mineral *silica*. Geyserite forms very slowly—only about 1/100-inch (1/4-mm) of this material is produced each year. Sometimes geyserite forms thin, colorful, lacelike sheets. It may also take the form of small pearly beads or larger objects called geyser eggs.

Other Kinds of Hot Springs

A hot spring that keeps bubbling away and giving off steam and water is called a *spouter.*

A *fumarole,* or steam vent, is the hottest of all hot springs. By the time the superheated water reaches the surface, all that is left is steam. Yellowstone's Black Growler roars like a den of angry lions and sends steam howling out at a

🐾 *Giant stepped terraces are formed by continuous deposits of the mineral travertine. Because travertine can build up at a rate of 20 inches (50 cm) a year, this mineral's outflow from hot springs can overwhelm trees.*

temperature as high as 284°F (140°C). A chemical called hydrogen sulfide gives a fumarole the unpleasant odor of a rotten egg.

When a hot pool has more dirt than water, it forms a bubbling *mud pot*. Mud pots are heated by steam and sputter like a simmering pot of dirty oatmeal. They may be less than 1 inch (2.5 cm) across or up to 30 feet (10 m) in diameter. While most are shallow, they may form craters up to 9 feet (3 m) deep. Like fumaroles, many mud pots contain hydrogen sulfide.

Some mud pots are better described as *paint pots* because they are vividly colored by minerals. One area of Yellowstone has a rainbow of mud pots that bubble with white, orange, and pink mud.

A *mud volcano* has a cone with mud bubbling inside. Whenever mud clogs the outlet vent, pressure builds up until it erupts, spewing mud in all directions.

The Valley of Geysers and Yellowstone both have many mud pots. These are bubbling and sputtering pools that contain a thick mixture of steaming dirt and water.

Strokkur Geyser in Iceland, which erupts every few minutes, throws a plume of steam and superheated water 65 to 130 feet (20 to 40 m) into the air.

Three

Geysers Galore

M ore than three-quarters of all geysers in the world can be found either at Kronotski National Park in Russia or Yellowstone National Park in the United States. Earth has two

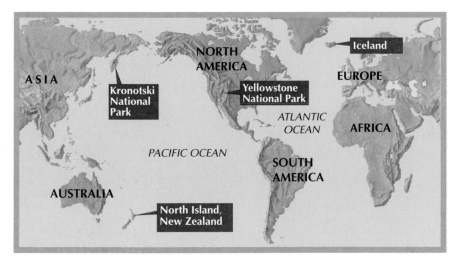

Nearly all of the world's geysers are located in four areas.

other major geyser hot spots. Both are located on small island nations—Iceland and New Zealand.

Geysers and Glaciers

The island of Iceland, which is smaller than New York State, is a land of fire and ice. Large glaciers lie next to steaming hot springs, geysers, and volcanoes. It was formed about 50 million years ago by volcanic outpourings and floods of molten magma. Today, Iceland is being pulled apart by a great chain of undersea volcanic mountains called the *Mid-Atlantic Ridge*.

Volcanoes buried deep beneath Iceland still erupt from time to time. In 1963, an undersea volcano south of Iceland erupted, forming a new island just 11 miles (18 km) away.

Of Iceland's 200 volcanoes, Mount Hekla is the most famous. It has been erupting about twice every 100 years since the year 1100. Two other active volcanoes, Katla and Grimsvotn, are almost completely buried beneath glacial ice. Both erupt from time to time and cause enormous floods—called "jokulhlaups"—that sweep away houses, people, and anything else in their path. These floods of water, ice chunks, and boulders race across the land at 60 miles (100 km) per hour.

Until a few decades ago, Iceland had about 100 active geysers. Today, only about two dozen are still erupting. The

Today, Iceland's Great Geyser isn't nearly so great as it was 100 years ago. At that time, it ejected a fountain of scalding water more than 200 feet (60 m) into the air.

largest and most famous of these is called Great Geyser. Scattered throughout Great Geyser's basin are about two dozen smaller geysers that erupt every now and then. In its heyday, Great Geyser regularly ejected a column of scalding water and steam more than 200 feet (60 m) into the air. Its 5-minute-long eruptions occurred about every 6 hours. But since the early 1900s, Great Geyser has gradually quieted down.

Iceland also has about 700 natural hot springs and many hot bubbling mud pools. Most of these are located along the Mid-Atlantic Ridge, which runs from north to south through the middle of Iceland. The water temperature in these especially hot springs reaches more than 158°F (70°C). In most cases, the water deep inside the hot springs boils violently, flashes into steam, and hisses skyward as misty jets. If shifting soil clogs the vent of one of these springs, a gurgling mud pool will form.

Iceland: Nature's Hothouse

Several years ago one Icelandic family decided to get free heat for their house by building it over a hot spring. Their plan was working well until one day when the kitchen floor cracked open, boiling water gushed out, and the entire house flooded. *Geothermal energy* is the term used to describe putting Earth's natural heat to work.

A tower of hot cloud rises from Iceland's Krafla geothermal power plant. Some 70 percent of Iceland's buildings are heated by scalding water from hot springs.

Today about 70 percent of Iceland's buildings are heated by the scalding water of hot springs. Almost every building in the capital city of Reykjavik is heated by water tapped from 1,000- to 2,000-foot (300- to 600-m) *boreholes* drilled into the ground.

Some of these boreholes are located 10 miles (15 km) away from Reykjavik, so the water is piped to the city. Water rising from the boreholes is about 220°F (105°C). By the time the water reaches factories or homes, it has dropped only a few degrees.

New Zealand's Thermal Treasures

At one time, the North Island of New Zealand had more than 200 active geysers and hot springs. From 1899 to 1904, a geyser named Waimangu, which means "Bird Water," gushed an astonishing 1,500 feet (460 m) into the air. It was the world's largest geyser.

For more than a century, the city of Rotorua lured tourists to visit its geysers, hot springs, and pools of boiling mud. But as in Iceland, New Zealand's geothermal network is running out of steam. Because earthquakes have shifted the ground and changed the structure of underground vents and water storage cavities, there are only about a dozen active geysers left in New Zealand.

A second factor has caused many of New Zealand's geysers to become inactive. Since the early 1960s, New Zealanders have been tapping into the underground geothermal vents that feed the geysers. A major geothermal project in Wairakei Valley on North Island involved drilling

Since the 1960s, New Zealand has lost many of its majestic geysers because they were tapped to provide steam to geothermal plants, like this one in Wairakei Valley on North Island. To save some of the remaining geysers, the government closed off many boreholes.

numerous boreholes. The steam and hot water released by these boreholes was piped to a nearby plant and used to generate electricity. The result of this drilling was a tremendous reduction in the area's geothermal activity. In the 1980s, the government closed off some of the boreholes in an effort to save the country's geysers.

Other geysers and small geyser fields are scattered throughout the world. One of these is in El Tatio, Chile. There may be as many as sixty-five additional geysers located among the Andes Mountains in South America.

There are also some geysers in Tibet, some along the African Rift Valley, and on New Britain Island in Papua New Guinea. They have also been found in Japan, the Azores, Thailand, Fiji, Indonesia, and Mexico. The geyser fields in these areas typically contain only two or three geysers.

Although the most spectacular geysers in the United States are certainly those at Yellowstone National Park, a few other geysers can be found in other parts of the country. Several small geysers spout along the Long Valley Caldera of California, and one discovered in 1990 erupts at Mickey Hot Springs in Oregon. Alaska has a few as well, as do the neighboring Aleutian Islands. The number of geysers in any geyser field is always changing. As new geysers form, old ones die.

Four

Geysers Under the Sea

I n 1977, scientists were surprised to find undersea geysers in the Pacific Ocean. Then in 1985, they found more geysers along the Mid-Atlantic Ridge, which is in the Atlantic Ocean. The Ridge, which runs from the North Atlantic Ocean to Antarctica, twists and turns along 46,000 miles (74,000 km) of ocean floor.

Today, ocean scientists called *oceanographers* believe that undersea geyser fields are common. These *hydrothermal vents* spout wherever hot molten rock wells up from beneath the ocean floor. The molten rock spews through openings made as great slabs of rock, called *plates,* are pulled apart.

As the molten rock cools, it hardens and builds new sections of sea floor. When cracks develop in this new sea floor, cold ocean water seeps into the cracks and comes into contact with hot rock. The water is heated under great pressure, and flashes into steam.

As the steam bursts toward the surface, it explosively pushes the water above it up through the sea floor as geysers. When the water is below the surface, it picks up minerals from the rock. As a result, the water around a deep-sea geyser field is unusually warm and contains more minerals than most deep-sea water. This special water is able to support a bizarre assortment of plant and animal life. In fact, some scientists think that the first life on Earth may have developed in deep-sea vents on the ocean floor.

Life Around a Black Smoker

One of the first scientists to investigate this remarkable undersea world was geologist Robert Ballard. In 1977, he lowered a small vehicle with a camera to the ocean floor near the Galapagos Islands, which are off the coast of South America. Scientists found it hard to believe what the photos showed—enormous clams, strange crabs, and giant tube worms with red plumes.

They also saw "chimneys" up to 165 feet (50 m) tall belching what looked like black smoke. The black "smoke" turned out to be clouds of hot minerals—iron, copper, silver, zinc, tin, cobalt, lead, and sulfur. As these minerals build up, they look

Giant tube worms are just one of the bizarre plants and animals that live around a deep-sea vent.

like colorful undersea chimneys. Scientists eventually realized that they were actually looking at powerful undersea geysers.

Some of the mineral chimneys, which are called black smokers, are shapeless clumps, while others are slim and tall. Still others have onion-shaped domes. These chimneys may

A hot deep-sea geyser chimney takes form as orange, green, or brown minerals turn solid when they mix with cool ocean water. Many such mineral chimneys have been discovered in both the Pacific and Atlantic oceans.

be orange, green, brown, or white, depending on the kinds of minerals they contain. The minerals that pour out of black smokers are hundreds of degrees hot—in some cases nearly 1,000°F (540°C).

During one expedition an oceanographer reported seeing "blizzards" of bacteria spewing from newly opened fissures and billowing 160 feet (50 m) high. He called these bacteria "snowblowers."

In 1985, a scientist named Peter Rona explored the seafloor in a Mir 1 Russian submarine. He was surprised to discover a huge undersea geyser field located 1,800 miles (2,900 km) east of Miami, Florida. It was the first geyser field ever discovered in the Atlantic Ocean. The field consists of dozens of black smokers perched atop the Mid-Atlantic Ridge, 2.5 miles (4 km) below the surface. Since that time, scientists have identified more than fifteen other hydrothermal vents.

As Rona explored the vent community near Florida, he observed a variety of astonishing undersea creatures, including a type of eyeless shrimp. He named the new species *Rimicavis exoculata,* which means "dweller in the rift without eyes."

Hydrothermal vents are oases in the vast ocean desert. They support an incredible diversity life. Ocean biologists are still trying to figure out how the more than 300 new *species* of organisms discovered in geyser *ecosystems* interact with one

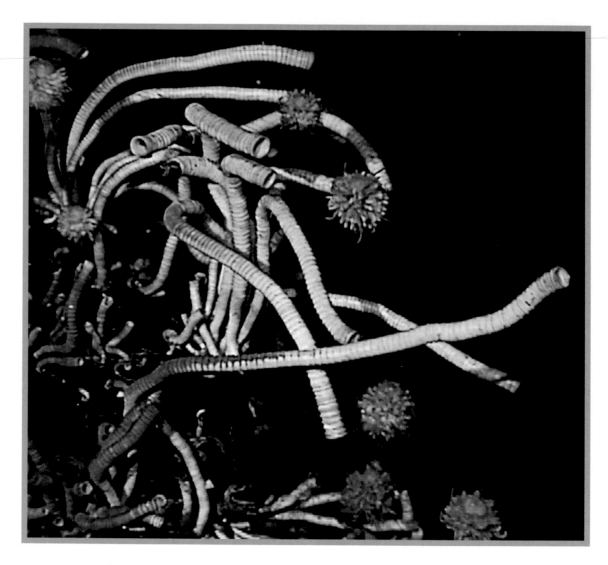

Life comes and goes quickly in a deep-sea vent community. Here, ping-pong-sized siphonophores are still trying to capture food among a colony of dying Jericho worms.

another. They also want to know how these organisms adapted to life at the bottom of the ocean.

The species living in undersea vent communities are unlike any other creatures on Earth. To begin with, they depend on energy from Earth's interior, not on energy from sunlight. The smallest of these organisms feed on *nutrients* in the mineral-rich water that erupts from the undersea geysers. Like any other ecosystem on Earth, the smaller organisms are hunted by larger ones.

The bacteria and other microscopic life forms in a deep-sea vent community are a food source for shrimp, clams, and limpets. Tube worms provide a safe home for the bacteria, and in exchange the bacteria supply them with the nutrients the tube worms need to survive. Blind crabs prey on the tube worms and other organisms. The zoarcid fish is at the top of the hydrothermal vent's food chain. It eats the crabs and many of the other animals that live in the water surrounding a deep-sea geyser.

Unlike most land communities, undersea vent communities come and go relatively quickly. That is because the vents are often changed or destroyed by sea floor movements. A typical vent community may last only 50 years or so. When *geological* forces destroy a vent, they also destroy the entire vent community.

Five

Inside Earth

bout 600 years ago, during the Middle Ages, many people believed that hell was located below Earth's surface. They thought that volcanoes were entrances to Earth's interior—and gateways to hell. According to popular local myths, the noises coming from deep within Iceland's Mount Hekla were supposedly the moans and screams of tormented human souls.

Empedocles, a Greek philosopher who lived about 2,400 years ago, thought that the center of Earth was made of molten rock and that this hot, liquid rock was the source of volcanic outpourings. Today we know that Empedocles was right.

In the past 100 years, nearly every square inch of our planet's surface has been explored. Yet just beneath our feet are vast unexplored regions—regions we will never see and may never fully understand.

Scientists cannot collect samples of material from Earth's center. The average distance to Earth's center is 3,959 miles (6,371 km), and we can drill holes only about 4 miles (6.5 km) deep. Those holes, and the deepest mines, show that the deeper we go, the hotter it gets.

Beneath Earth's Crust

Earth's *crust,* the layer of rock that we walk on, extends about 6 miles (9.6 km) beneath the oceans and about 37 miles (60 km) beneath the continents. Most of the continents are made up of a granite-type rock. Temperatures within the crust go up to about 1,800°F (980°C).

Beneath the crust is a much thicker layer of rock called the *mantle.* The mantle, which is about 1,800 miles (2,900 km) thick, contains large quantities of iron and magnesium. Because the rock that makes up the mantle is closer to the center of Earth than the rock in the crust, it is under more pressure.

Mantle rock is squeezed this way and that, like toothpaste in an uncapped tube. Since the *molecules* in the rock are under so much pressure, they are forced to move closer together. As the molecules are compressed, they give off energy in the form

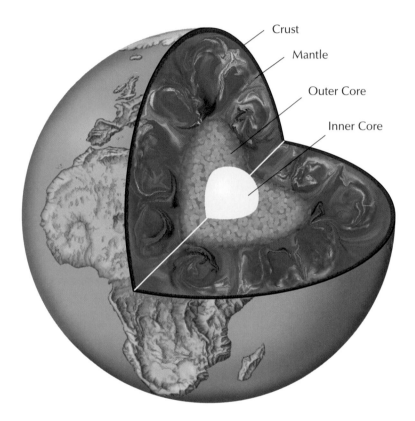

Crust

Mantle

Outer Core

Inner Core

Scientists have divided Earth's interior into four layers: the inner core, the outer core, the mantle, and the crust. Each layer has unique physical characteristics.

of heat. As a result, the innermost regions of the mantle reach temperatures of up to 7,500°F (4,150°C).

Below the mantle is Earth's *core* region. The inner layer of the core, which is about 800 miles (1,300 km) thick, seems to be a large ball of solid iron and nickel. It is surrounded by an outer layer of liquid iron and nickel. The outer core is about 1,400 miles (2,250 km) thick. The temperature at Earth's center may be as high as 7,000°F (3,870°C).

Rafts in a Sea of Magma

Earth and the rest of our Solar System was formed about 4.6 billion years ago. At first, only millions of grains of dust and rock orbited around the new sun. When these tiny particles collided, they sometimes stuck together. As more and more dust and rock combined, they formed larger bodies called *planetesimals*.

Eventually, the largest planetesimals, which contained large amounts of silicate materials, combined and became planets. The smaller planetesimals, which contained lots of heavier materials—iron and nickel, became *meteoroids*. Young Earth continued to grow by sweeping up more and more large planetesimals. All the while Earth was bombarded by tens of thousands of meteoroids. These impacts played an important role in forming our planet because they provided it with iron and other material heavier than the rocky silicates.

Eventually, the hot, soupy ball of molten rock and metals that made up primitive Earth began to cool. The lighter silicate materials floated up to the surface of the planet, while the heavier iron and nickel materials sank into the core region.

From time to time, large meteoroids continued to smash into Earth's solidifying crust. Scientists believe that these collisions broke the crust into large chunks.

Throughout our planet's history, the continents have drifted about in the sea of molten rock that makes up the mantle. And they are still moving today. What keeps the continents drifting like rafts in a sea of magma? It is the tremendous heat deep within our planet. As the molten rock of the mantle and outer core churns, its heat is carried toward Earth's surface. This is the heat that boils the water that fuels geysers.

Six

How Geysers Work

The Mid-Atlantic Ridge keeps the surface of Earth active. You have already seen that it is the home of many undersea geysers. In addition, a rift valley—a deep trench along the top of the Ridge—gushes molten rock. This magma spills down the slopes of the Ridge.

As the magma cools, new material is added to the ocean floor. This causes the seafloor to spread out on both sides of the Ridge. Because the ocean floor is spreading, the United States and Europe are being pushed apart at a rate of about 1 inch (2.5 cm) each year. As you learned in Chapter 5, this crustal motion, called *continental drift,* is possible because the continents are floating like rafts on a sea of dense mantle rock.

Earth's crust appears to be broken into six major slabs of rock, or plates, and about a dozen smaller ones. Sometimes the edges of two neighboring plates grind together. When they do, something has to happen along their edges.

For instance, seafloor spreading pushes the Nazca Plate eastward against the South American Plate. The two plates collide along the coasts of Chile and Peru in South America.

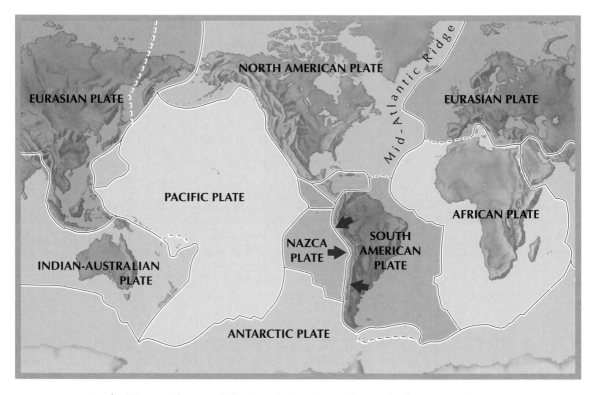

As the Nazca Plate and the South American Plate collide against one another, the Nazca Plate is pushed down into the hot mantle rock and melts. As a result, this area of the world has many active volcanoes and geysers.

The lighter rock of the South American Plate rides up over the heavier basaltic rock of the Nazca Plate. At the same time, the edge of the Nazca Plate is pushed down into the hot mantle rock, and the heat of the mantle rock melts the leading edge of the Nazca Plate. Some of this newly melted rock will eventually force its way up through the South American Plate to the surface. The result may be volcanic activity and the formation of geyser fields.

To Gush or Not to Gush

In 1880, Robert W. Bunsen, a German chemist, suggested that a heat source deep inside Earth warms the water that erupts from a geyser. Today, we know that the heat source—magma—comes from the melting of continental plates as one slides over another.

Besides heat and lots of water, said Bunsen, two other conditions are necessary for a hot spring to become a geyser—an underground plumbing system and the right kind of water chemistry.

The plumbing system must consist of a tubular vent filled with water nearly to ground level. Water from rain and melting snow seeps into the ground and fills the long tube. At some point mineral deposits make the tube so narrow that the tube acts like a nozzle. Magma deep underground heats

the solid rock above it, and the solid rock heats the water in the lower part of the tube. Pressure below the "nozzle" builds up so much that when the water and steam finally erupt, they are thrust high into the air.

At the beginning of an eruption cycle, the water at the bottom of the tube is heated by surrounding rocks. The water does not boil, at least not right away, because the weight of the water above it keeps the water under high pressure. The temperature of the water at the bottom of the tube continues to rise until it becomes hot enough to boil, despite the pressure.

Bubbles of volcanic gas in the now boiling water cause the water to expand and exert pressure on the water above it. Eventually, the water at the top of the tube spills out. Because the tube contains less water, the pressure being applied to the water at the bottom of the tube decreases.

As the pressure decreases, more and more of the water begins to boil. In turn, more and more water spills out of the vent at ground level. At the same time, steam from the boiling water causes more and more water to boil. Soon, all the water in the tube begins to boil and large quantities of steam rise to the surface, and the geyser spouts. When

Grotto Geyser in Yellowstone's Upper Geyser Basin has built up a chaotic clump of sinter, which is a deposit of silica. Similar deposits line the tubes of a geyser's plumbing system and keep the tubes watertight.

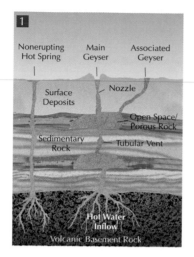

Noneupting
Hot Spring | Main Geyser | Associated Geyser

Surface Deposits — Nozzle

Open Space/
Porous Rock

Sedimentary Rock — Tubular Vent

Hot Water Inflow

Volcanic Basement Rock

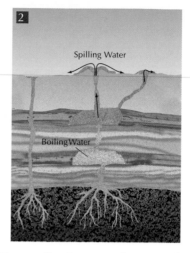

Spilling Water

Boiling Water

At the beginning of the eruption cycle, water at the bottom of the tubular vent is heated, but does not boil because it is under too much pressure.

Eventually, the water begins to boil and expand. Some water spills out of the tube and the pressure inside decreases.

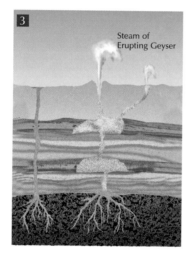

Steam of Erupting Geyser

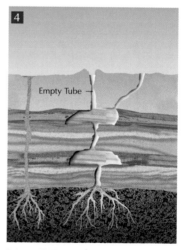

Empty Tube

Soon, all the water boils and large quantities of steam are forced up the tube. The geyser erupts.

When all the water has left the tube, the geyser stops spouting. Underground water sources will eventually refill the tube, and the cycle will begin again.

all of the water and steam have left the tube, the geyser stops spouting. Although the geyser seems quiet at the surface, the eruption cycle has started all over again about 2 miles (3.2 km) underground. As soon as the tube refills with water from surrounding pockets of ground water, it will be heated until it gushes another mighty tower of water and steam.

A geyser's plumbing tubes are lined with geyserite—the delicate, flaky material you learned about in Chapter 2. The geyserite lining is responsible for the narrowing that causes water pressure to build up inside the tube. Without this pressure, the water would just leak out the vent rather than gush up the tube.

Recently, scientists have found that the movement of a drop of water through one complete eruption cycle may take at least 500 years. That is the amount of time it takes for a drop of rain to seep through the ground to a deep underground water reservoir, drain into a geyser tube, be heated and spout into the air, and then fall to the ground again as rain. The next time you see a geyser erupt, chances are that the gushing water fell as rain around the time Columbus set sail for the New World.

Some geysers vent continuously, their steam forming endless swirling clouds of water. But eventually all geysers must die as their plumbing systems, which are nearly always shared with other geysers, change over time.

Seven

Geysers in Danger

N o geyser skips an eruption. If a geyser doesn't gush on schedule, it is probably because its water and heat are being channeled elsewhere. The underground plumbing systems of geysers are complex, connected, and shared. The eruption of one geyser in a geyser field affects all the other geysers in that field.

In 1990, Jubillee Grotto, one of the most famous geysers in Russia's Kronotski National Park, was extremely active. It erupted up to eight times a day. By 1995, it was steaming, but quiet.

Geysers are also affected by earthquakes, which are fairly common in volcanic areas. Even a slight shaking of the ground in a geyser field may change the structure of the plumbing system that feeds the geysers.

In 1959, a major earthquake shook Yellowstone National Park and caused many geysers to erupt with a vigor never seen before or since. A number of old, quiet hot springs suddenly burst into activity. Some of the geysers created by that earthquake continue to gush today; others have returned to their quiet gurgling.

Human Causes of Geyser Change

As you learned in Chapter 3, human activity can alter geyser activity. In fact, we know more about the human causes of geyser deaths than we do about natural causes. Most of New Zealand's geysers have been lost due to steam "mining" in order to produce electricity. Drilling into a geyser's plumbing system can damage hot springs at least 25 miles (40 km) away.

"Gone, too, are the geysers of Beowawa and Steamboat Springs, Nevada, in the United States," according to geologist Scott Bryan. "Recent human activity has doomed most geysers to extinction."

These geyser fields were once so beautiful that they were proposed as the site of a national park. As so often happens, when humans have to make a choice between preserving nature or heating their living room, they choose to harness the source of that beauty to generate electricity.

Fortunately, that has not happened on the Kamchatka Peninsula. The Russians are making every effort to preserve Dolina Geizerov. Foreign visitors were not even allowed in this spectacular geyser field before 1990. Even today, relatively few visitors are admitted.

Much to their credit, the Russians are determined to protect their remarkable geyser field, which is accessible only by helicopter. According to Scott Bryan, "Dolina Geizerov is the only large geyser field in the world to remain in a totally natural condition."

"Geysers," he adds, "are a rare and endangered geological species."

———<><>———

GLOSSARY

algae—single-celled or multicelled organisms that normally make their own food using energy from sunlight.

bacteria—single-celled organisms that have no nucleus. They vary widely in form as well as in oxygen and nutritional requirements. Many types cause disease in plants and animals.

boreholes—a hole drilled in the ground to release geothermal energy.

continental drift—the slow movement of the continents due to the changing position of the plates that make up the surface of Earth.

core—the central region of Earth. It is composed of iron and nickel and is divided into two regions—a solid inner core and a liquid outer core.

crust—the thin layer of rock that covers the surface of our planet.

ecosystem—a community of organisms plus all the physical conditions of their environment.

fumarole—a ground vent in a geothermal area that gives off steam and other gases because very little groundwater is present.

geological—having to do with Earth.

geothermal energy—energy tapped from hot water or steam in a volcanic region. The water is heated by molten rock deposits below Earth's surface.

geyser—a type of hot spring that intermittently erupts a column of steam and hot water. The word means "to gush."

geyserite—a brittle mineral deposit that forms around a hot spring. Geyserite also lines the vent tubes of geysers and is the agent that makes them pressure tight.

hot spring—any naturally occurring pool of water heated by geothermal energy. A hot spring may be quiet, or it may erupt as a geyser.

hydrothermal vents—underwater geysers.

magma—fluid rock material that forms deep below Earth's surface. It is capable of forcing its way up through solid rock. When it flows out over the surface, it is called lava.

mantle—the layer of rock beneath Earth's crust. It is made of iron and magnesium mixed with silicates. Because the mantle rock is under great pressure from the weight of rock above, the upper mantle is hot and behaves more like putty than a solid. The lower portion of the mantle is rigid.

meteoroid—a chunk of rock or metals that travels through space and sometimes enters Earth's atmosphere.

Mid-Atlantic Ridge—a volcanic mountain range located in the middle of the Atlantic Ocean.

molecule—a group of atoms that form the smallest unit of a substance that can exist and retain its chemical properties.

mud geyser—a geyser with a crater that is filled with fuming, sulfurous, bubbling mud. Mud geysers, like water geysers, erupt when steam pressure from below is released explosively.

mud pot—a hot spring filled with boiling mud.

mud volcano—a volcano, usually small, that forms when a hot spring becomes clogged with soil. When the hot spring erupts, mud spills out. Cones of solidified mud have built up around some mud volcanoes.

nutrient—a mineral element or compound that plants, animals, and most bacteria and fungi cannot make for themselves.

oceanographers—scientists who study the ocean.

Pacific Rim of Fire—a region of large-scale volcanic activity that falls along the edges of the Pacific plate.

paint pot—a mud pot that contains minerals that make the mud colorful.

planetesimals—chunks of rock and metals swept up by Earth during its formation about 4.6 billion years ago.

plates—rock platforms that form Earth's crust. There are six major plates and about a dozen smaller ones. The continents, along with sections of the ocean floor, are pushed about like giant rafts of stone floating in a sea of molten rock.

silica—the material from which quartz, sand, flint, and other white or colorless minerals are composed. It contains the elements silicon and oxygen.

species—any one kind of animal or plant group, each member of which is like every other member in certain important ways. All populations of such a group are capable of interbreeding and producing healthy offspring.

spouter—a hot spring that gushes steam and water.

RESOURCES

BOOKS

Bryan, T. Scott. Geysers: *What They Are and How They Work.* Niwot, CO: Roberts Rinehart, 1990.

———. *The Geysers of Yellowstone.* Boulder: Colorado Associated University Press, 1986.

Cottrell, W. H. *Born of Fire.* Niwot, CO: Roberts Rinehart, 1987.

Gallant, Roy A. *Restless Earth.* New York: Franklin Watts, 1986.

Marler, George D. *The Story of Old Faithful Geyser.* Yellowstone Park, WY: Yellowstone Library and Museum Association, 1963.

MAGAZINE ARTICLES

Bryan, T. Scott. "The Valley of the Geysers." *Earth* (July 1992), pp. 20–29.

Jordan, Robert Paul. "New Zealand: The Last Utopia?" *National Geographic* (May 1987), pp. 654–681.

Levathes, Louise E. "Iceland: Life Under the Glaciers." *National Geographic* (February 1987), pp. 184–215.

Lutz, Richard A. "Rebirth of a Deep-Sea Vent." *National Geographic* (November 1994), pp. 114–126.

Rona, Peter A. "Deep-Sea Geysers of the Atlantic." *National Geographic* (October 1992), pp. 105–109.

ORGANIZATIONS

Geyser Observation and Study Association
P.O. Box 2852
Apple Valley, CA 92370

This organization provides current, accurate information about geysers to the public and publishes a bimonthly newsletter about geysers.

WEB SITES

Due to the changeable nature of the Internet, sites appear and disappear very quickly. These resources offered useful information on geysers at the time of publication.

About Geysers is a page that provides information about geysers around the world and describes how they function. It's address is

http://www.wku.edu./www/geoweb/geyser/about2.html.

Activity of Selected Yellowstone Geysers lists the eruption schedule of the geysers in Yellowstone National Park. A map shows the location of each geyser and geyser field. It can be reached at

http://www.internet.com/yellowstone/geytable.htm.

Yellowstone Geysers is an excerpt from the Yellowstone Journal, which is published five times a year by the public information office at Yellowstone National Park. It's address is

http://www.wyoming.com/~yellowstonejournal/YellowstoneGeysers.html.

INDEX

Italicized page numbers indicate illustrations.

ABOUT THE AUTHOR

Roy A. Gallant has been called "one of the deans of American science writers for children" by *School Library Journal.* He has written more than eighty books for children on topics including astronomy, earth science, and evolution. Gallant has worked at the American Museum of Natural History and been a member of the faculty of the Hayden Planetarium. He is currently the director of the Southworth Planetarium at the University of Southern Maine, where he also holds an adjuct full professorship. Gallant lives in Rangeley, Maine.